CHINESE NEW YEAR

BY JUDITH JANGO-COHEN
ILLUSTRATIONS BY JASON CHIN

On My Own
HOLIDAYS

Carolrhoda Books, Inc./Minneapolis

The author thanks Eddy Lin, president of the American Chinese Art Society, for generously sharing his time and expertise.

Text copyright © 2005 by Judith Jango-Cohen
Illustrations copyright © 2005 by Jason Chin

This book is available in two editions:
Library binding by Carolrhoda Books, Inc., a division of Lerner Publishing Group
Soft cover by First Avenue Editions, an imprint of Lerner Publishing Group
241 First Avenue North
Minneapolis, MN 55401 U.S.A.

Website address: www.carolrhodabooks.com

Library of Congress Cataloging-in-Publication Data

Jango-Cohen, Judith.
    Chinese New Year / by Judith Jango-Cohen ;
  illustrations by Jason Chin.
      p.   cm. — (On my own holidays)
     ISBN: 1–57505–653–4 (lib. bdg. : alk. paper)
     ISBN: 1–57505–763–8 (pbk. : alk. paper)
     1. Chinese New Year. I. Chin, Jason, 1978– II. Title. III. Series.
GT4905.J35 2005
394.261—dc22   2004004472

Manufactured in the United States of America
1 2 3 4 5 6 – DP – 10 09 08 07 06 05

To Shannon Barefield, editor,
for the skill and dedication she brings
to all her projects
—J. J. C.

For my parents
—J. C.

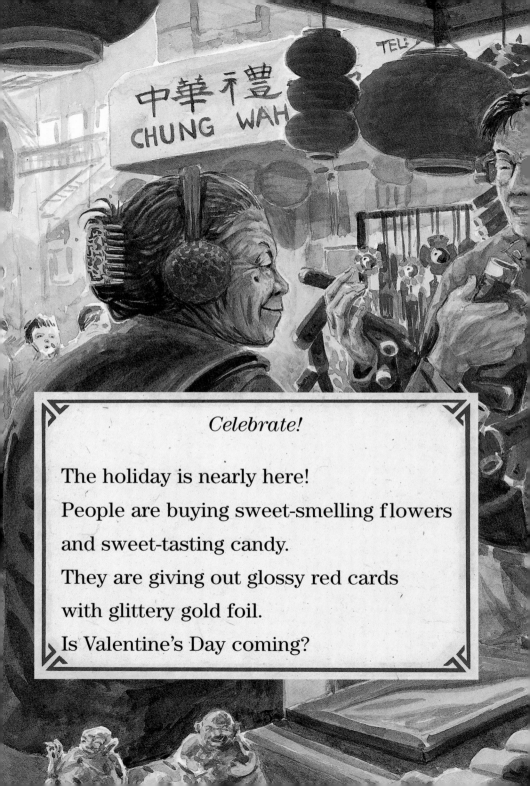

Celebrate!

The holiday is nearly here!
People are buying sweet-smelling flowers
and sweet-tasting candy.
They are giving out glossy red cards
with glittery gold foil.
Is Valentine's Day coming?

Children are trying on costumes.

One child is a lion.

She pulls a string to make its eyes
twinkle and blink.

Is Halloween about to begin?

Soon firecrackers will pop.

TAT-A-TAT! SNAP!

Fireworks will burst in the black sky.

BANG! KABOOM!

Shiny balls will bloom and glisten.

They flash and then fizzle.

Is it the Fourth of July?

This exciting holiday is Chinese New Year.

Have you ever celebrated it?

You do not need to live in China.

You do not even need to be Chinese.

Chinese New Year is an important holiday
in Chinese communities all over the world.

It is also called the Spring Festival.

It begins on a different date each year.

The date is based on the traditional
Chinese calendar.

The holiday always begins
in January or February.

And it always begins with
the first new moon of the year.

How can you tell when the moon is new?

No light brightens its face.

A new moon is as dark as a shadow.

On this new moon night,
15 days of celebrating begin.
Chinese New Year is too important
to last for just one day.
For 15 days,
people celebrate in many ways.
They celebrate quietly,
remembering days that have passed.

They also remember family and friends
who have died.
People celebrate with noisy excitement too.
Dancers leap to beating drums.
Rumbling parades stream
through the streets.
People cheer.
A new year is here.

Dusting and Decorating

The Spring Festival is a busy beginning
to the new year.
But the weeks before are busy too.
There is so much to do before the holiday.
Some families prepare for the new year
with a ceremony to the Kitchen God.
The Kitchen God carefully watches each
family during the year.
Then, one week before the new year,
he travels to heaven.
There he reports to the Jade Emperor.
The Kitchen God tells the Jade Emperor
about each family's good and bad deeds.

Before the Kitchen God leaves,
families gather at his altar.
The altar displays a picture
of the Kitchen God.
Sweet-smelling incense and candles
may be burning.
Families offer the Kitchen God
honey, chewy candies,
and sweet, sticky rice cakes.
These sweet treats will put him
in a good mood.
Better yet, the gooey food may prevent him
from opening his mouth.
He will not be able to say anything bad.
Then the Jade Emperor will bless
the family with a year of happiness.

Families also prepare for a good
new year by cleaning the house.
All the bad luck from last year
gets washed away with the dirt.
Paint! Polish! Dust and scrub!
Don't forget under the bed!
When gritty grime is gone,
good luck can come in.
To welcome the good luck,
people hang a scarlet banner on
each side of their front door.
Each banner displays a poem
written in black or gold.
These pairs of poems
are called spring couplets.
They carry wishes for joy in the new year.

"Spring has arrived
and good luck has come."
"May happiness and
fortune flow like
mountain streams."

Inside, people brighten
their homes with flowers.
They buy orchids and peonies with
pretty petals and sweet scents.
Flowers are an important symbol
during Chinese New Year.
A symbol is an object that
stands for an idea.

Flowers stand for the idea of beginnings.

Can you imagine why?

Flowers make seeds.

Seeds are the beginnings

of new flowers.

If your flowers bloom

on New Year's Day,

that is a sign of good luck.

Each home looks beautiful

with banners and flowers.

But people want to look good too.

Choose some colorful new clothes.

Red is best.

It is the color of happiness.

Be sure to get a haircut.

A new haircut will make you look different.

If you are lucky, the evil spirits from last

year will not realize who you are!

Now you are set to welcome the new year.
On the Chinese calendar,
each year is named for one of 12 animals.
These 12 animals are called
the Chinese zodiac.
The new year could be the Year of the Rat
or the Rabbit, the Dog or the Dragon.
An old Chinese teaching says that
people are like the zodiac animal
of their birth year.
Those born in the Year of the Snake
are quiet and wise.
People are quick and cheerful if they
were born in the Year of the Horse.
Which year are we celebrating now?

THE CHINESE ZODIAC

RAT
2008, 1996

OX
2009, 1997

TIGER
2010, 1998

PIG
2007, 1995

RABBIT
2011, 1999

DOG
2006, 1994

DRAGON
2012, 2000

ROOSTER
2017, 2005

SNAKE
2013, 2001

MONKEY
2016, 2004

SHEEP
2015, 2003

HORSE
2014, 2002

23

The Family Feast

The weather is chilly in most places
during Chinese New Year.
But on New Year's Eve,
the kitchen is always warm.
Duck is roasting.
Fish is steaming.

Noodles and dumplings bubble in big pots.
Dumplings are stuffed with spicy meat.
Sometimes a coin is hidden in
one of the dumplings.
If you find the coin, you will be
lucky all year.

New Year's Eve dishes are
not only delicious.
Each dish is a symbol of a wish
for the new year.
Duck stands for happiness.
Fish is a symbol of surplus,
or having more than enough.
Noodles give long life.
Dumplings bring riches
and family togetherness.

Togetherness is what makes
New Year's Eve so special.
Grandparents and aunts and uncles
may all live in different places.
But on New Year's Eve,
they gather around one table.
Sometimes a family member
is not able to be present.
That person is not forgotten.
A place is set at the table for anyone
who is missing.

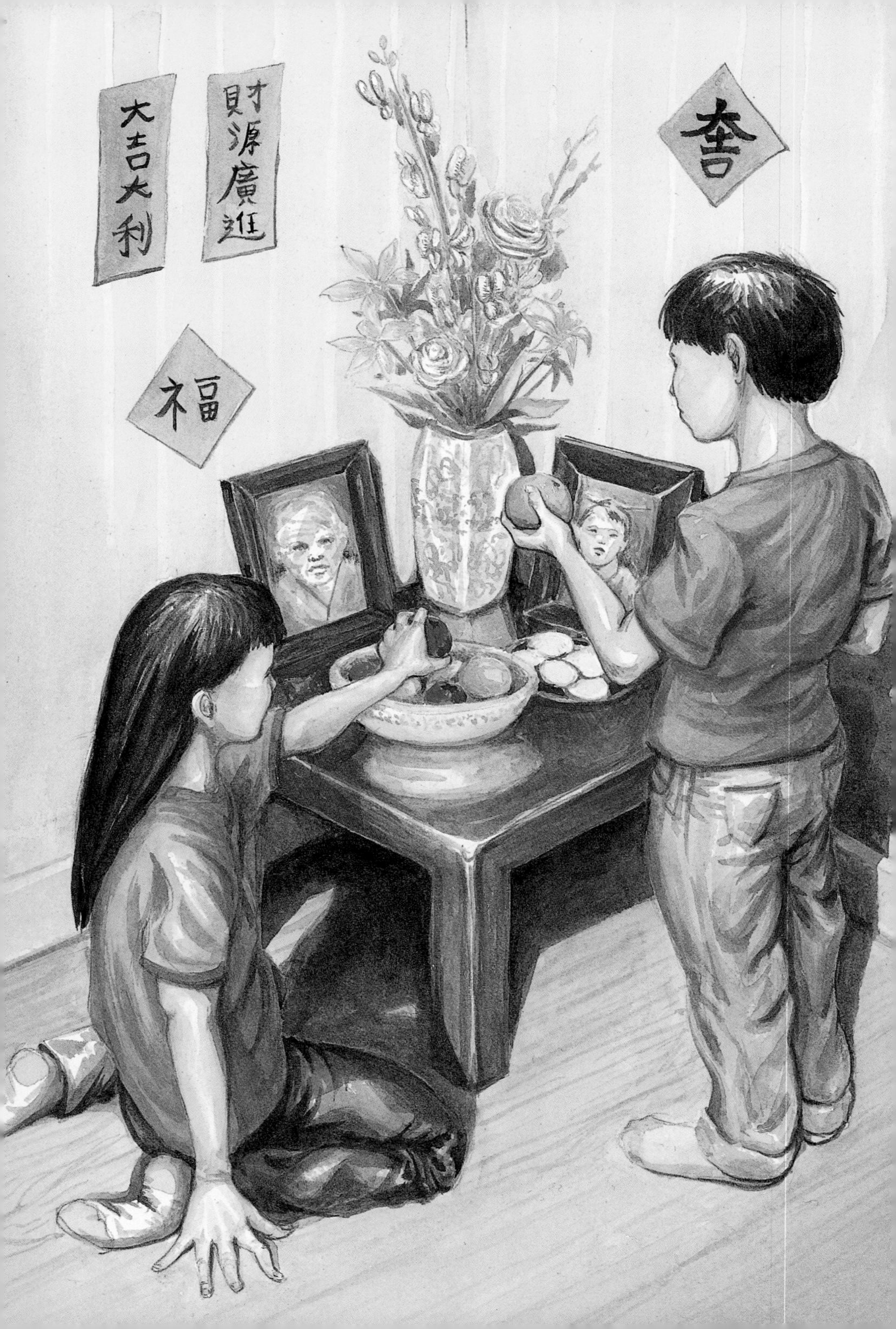
大吉大利
財源廣進
福

Some family members are missing
because they have died.
These relatives are remembered
in a different way.
The family sets up an altar for them.
The altar may display spring couplets,
candles, flowers, and pictures
of the relatives.
Families offer food to the
spirits of the relatives.
This food is later eaten by the family.
Bowls of oranges and red apples
are also set out.
The red is for happiness.
Oranges are a symbol of wealth
and good fortune.

After the meal, everyone nibbles
on candies and fruit.
Grown-ups tell stories.
"Remember when Grandpa broke a tooth on
the lucky coin in his dumpling?"
Children laugh and listen.
They learn about the family
before they were born.
Everyone stays up to say good-bye
to the old year.
Little ones struggle against yawns
and drooping eyelids.
They do not want to miss
the midnight excitement.
Sometimes children fall asleep.
But they wake up with a start at midnight.
BING! PING! POW!

Firecrackers explode.

Fireworks screech and burst open

with a booming blast.

The midnight sky is alive with light.

Chinese New Year comes in
with a roaring racket.
An old story tells us why.
Many, many years ago,
a beast lived in China.
Every New Year's Eve,
it raged through villages.

It plucked up people
and gulped them down.
Then villagers discovered that loud
sounds terrified the monster.
Since then, earsplitting noise
has been a custom
of Chinese New Year.

A quiet ceremony takes place
before bedtime.
People welcome back the Kitchen God.
He has returned from his visit
with the Jade Emperor.
People place food on his altar.
They say prayers in his honor.
Then, after the feast, fireworks, and
prayers, it is finally time for sleep.

Lions and Lanterns

When people wake up on New Year's Day,
they are careful about how they behave.
Some believe that whatever happens
on this day will keep happening
all year long.
People try to be patient.
They do favors for each other.
They do not say words like *sick* and *sad*.
The new year has to start off just right.

New Year's Day is spent visiting
relatives and friends.
It is a time for favorite foods
and family fun.
Families exchange presents like
peach blossoms and pussy willows.

They also give gifts of candy,
fruit, and rice cakes.
Grown-ups hand children
red and gold envelopes.
What is inside?
Lucky money!

After New Year's Day, there are still two
more weeks of Chinese New Year.
Each family celebrates in its own way.
So does each city.
Some places hold drum-thumping,
stilt-walking, somersaulting parades.

Acrobats tumble.

Bass drums rumble.

Children perch on their
parents' shoulders.

They clap for crazy clowns.

They cheer as flashy floats glide by.

Dancers dress up as lions.
These lions are not plain yellow
like real lions.
New Year lions may be purple,
pink, green, and gold.
They are trimmed with tassels
and speckled with sequins.

One dancer wears the back
of the costume.
The other wears the head.
This dancer pulls strings to wiggle
the lion's ears and light up its eyes.
When the lion opens its mouth wide,
you can see the dancer's head inside!

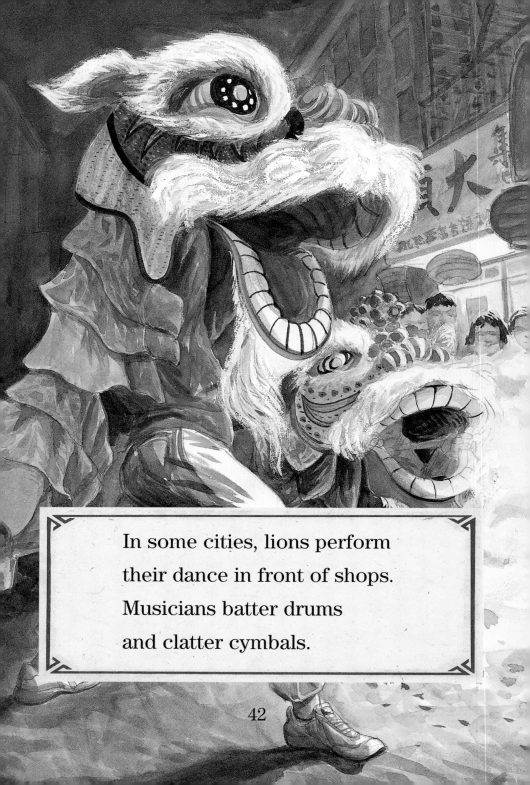

In some cities, lions perform
their dance in front of shops.
Musicians batter drums
and clatter cymbals.

42

Store owners set off strings
of red firecrackers.
The smoky explosions are meant
to chase off evil spirits.
This brings shopkeepers good luck
in the coming year.

Lions are not the only animals that
dance during Chinese New Year.
Slithery dragons swerve and weave
through the streets.
First the dragon's head appears,
with glowing eyes and glinting teeth.
Next comes its back,
with slinky stripes and shiny scales.

Where is the dragon's tail?
In the San Francisco parade,
it ends more than 200 feet
behind the head.
One hundred people bring
this dragon to life.
They stand inside the costume
and prop it up with poles.

After 15 days of prayers, parades,
fireworks, and feasts,
Chinese New Year ends.
The last celebration is called
the Lantern Festival.
Lanterns decorate doorways.
People carry them in parades.
There are gleaming globes.
There are zodiac animals made
from paper, silk, or glass.
In cold places, some lanterns
are cut from blocks of ice.
Chinese New Year always ends
on the night of a full moon.
A full moon is round and bright.
Moonbeams mingle with lantern lights.
Chinese New Year is ending.
But a new year of fun has just begun.

Glossary

Chinese New Year: a 15-day celebration that begins between the end of January and the end of February

Chinese zodiac: the animals named for each year in the 12-year cycle of the Chinese calendar

incense: a substance that is burned to give off a pleasing smell. Incense is often burned during ceremonies.

Jade Emperor: the highest of all gods in the Taoist religion, one of the main religions in China

Kitchen God: the god in the Taoist religion who lives all year with each family. Also called the God of the Hearth.

symbol: an object that stands for an idea